Trevor Noah: A

Trevor Noah is a South African comedian, television and radio host and actor. He currently hosts The Daily Show, a late-night television talk show on Comedy Central.

Early life and family

Trevor Noah was born in Johannesburg, South Africa. His mother, Patricia Nombuyiselo Noah, is of mixed Xhosa and Jewish ancestry, and his father, Robert, is of Swiss German ethnicity. Noah spent his early youth in the private school of Maryvale College, a Catholic school in Johannesburg. His parents' relationship was illegal at the time of his birth under apartheid. His mother was jailed and fined by the South African white minority government, and his father later moved back to Switzerland. Noah was raised by his mother and maternal grandmother, Nomalizo Frances Noah. During his childhood, he attended Roman Catholic church every Sunday.

Noah's mixed-race ancestry, his experiences growing up in Soweto, and his observations about race and ethnicity are leading themes in his comedy.

Career

When he was 18, Noah had a starring role on the South African soap opera Isidingo. He then began hosting his own radio show Noah's Ark on Gauteng's leading youth radio station, YFM. Noah went on to host an educational program, Run The Adventure on SABC 2. In 2007, he hosted The Real Goboza, a gossip show on SABC 1, and Siyadlala, a sports show which also aired on the SABC. In 2008, Noah co-hosted, alongside Pabi Moloi, The Amazing Date and was a Strictly Come Dancing contestant in season 4. In 2009, he hosted the 3rd Annual South Africa Film and Television Awards and co-hosted alongside Eugene Khoza on The Axe Sweet Life, a reality competition series. In 2010, Noah hosted the 16th annual South African Music Awards and also hosted Tonight with Trevor Noah on MNet. In 2010, Noah also became a spokesperson and consumer protection agent for Cell C, South Africa's third largest cellular provider.

Noah dropped his radio show and acting to focus on comedy, and has performed with South African comedians such as David Kau, Kagiso Lediga, Riaad Moosa, Darren Simpson, Marc Lottering, Barry Hilton and Nik Rabinowitz, international comedians such as Paul Rodriguez, Carl Barron, Dan Ilic and Paul Zerdin, and as the opening act for Gabriel Iglesias in November 2007 and Canadian comedian Russell Peters on his South African tour.

Noah has performed all over South Africa in The Blacks Only Comedy Show, the Heavyweight Comedy Jam, the Vodacom Campus Comedy Tour, the Cape Town International Comedy Festival, the Jozi Comedy Festival and Bafunny Bafunny. His stand-up comedy specials in South Africa include The Daywalker, Crazy Normal, That's Racist, and It's My Culture.

In 2011, he moved to the United States. On 6 January 2012, Noah became the first South African stand-up comedian to appear on The Tonight Show; and, on 17 May 2013, he became the first to appear on Late Show with David Letterman. Noah was the subject of the 2012 documentary You Laugh But It's True. The same year, he starred in the one-man comedy show Trevor Noah: The Racist which was based on his similarly titled South African special That's Racist. On 12 September, Noah was the Roastmaster in a Comedy Central

Roast of South African Afrikaans singer Steve Hofmeyr. In 2013, he performed the comedy special Trevor Noah: African American. On 11 October 2013, he was a guest on BBC Two's comedy panel show QI. On 29 November 2013, he was a panelist on Channel 4 game show 8 Out of 10 Cats and appeared on Sean Lock's team in 8 Out of 10 Cats Does Countdown on 12 September 2014.

In December 2014, Noah became a recurring contributor on The Daily Show. In March 2015, Comedy Central announced that Noah would succeed Jon Stewart as host of The Daily Show; his tenure began on 28 September 2015.

Controversy and allegations of antisemitism

Within hours of his being announced as Stewart's successor, attention was drawn on the Internet to several jokes that Noah had made through his Twitter account, which were criticized as being offensive to women or Jews. Noah responded by tweeting, "To reduce my views to a handful of jokes that didn't land is not a true reflection of my character, nor my evolution as a comedian." Comedy Central stood behind Noah, saying in a statement, "Like many comedians, Trevor Noah pushes boundaries; he is provocative and spares no one, himself included... To judge him or his comedy based on a handful of jokes is unfair. Trevor is a talented comedian with a bright future at Comedy Central." Mary Kluk, chairperson of the South African Jewish Board of Deputies, said that the jokes were not signs of anti-Jewish prejudice and that they were part of Noah's style of comedy. She stated, "The SAJBD wishes him all the success and wisdom that he will require in his new position, and is confident that he will do our country proud."

Influences

Noah has said of his comedic influences, "The kings are indisputable. Richard Pryor; Cosby; for me personally I didn't know of him before I started comedy but Eddie Murphy changed my view on the thing and I definitely look up to him as a comedic influence. Chris Rock in terms of the modern black comedian and Dave Chappelle. Those are the guys that have laid the foundation and have moved the yardstick for all comedians, not just Black comedians." He also cited Jon Stewart as an influence, following his appointment to succeed Stewart as host of The Daily Show.

Personal life

Noah is a polyglot; he speaks several languages including English, Xhosa, Zulu, Sotho, Afrikaans, and German.

In 1992, Noah's mother was married to Ngisaveni Shingange, and while married they had two sons. She divorced him in 1996. In 2009, after she became engaged to Sfiso Khoza, Shingange shot her in the back and face, stopping when the gun jammed; she survived. When Noah later confronted him on the phone about the shooting, Shingange threatened his life, prompting Noah to leave Johannesburg for Los Angeles. In 2011, Shingange was convicted of attempted murder, and sentenced the following year to three years of correctional supervision. Noah stated that he hoped the attention surrounding the incident would help the domestic abuse problem in South Africa: "For years my mother reached out to police for help with domestic abuse, and nothing was ever done. This is the norm in South Africa. Dockets went missing and cases never went to court."

Noah has described himself as being progressive and having a global perspective. However, he has clarified that he considers himself a "progressive person", but not a "political progressive" and prefers not to be categorized as either right or left in the context of US partisanship.

He has been in a relationship with model Jordyn Taylor since 2015.

Awards

The Daily Show is an American news satire and talk show television program, which airs each Monday through Thursday on Comedy Central and on The Comedy Network in Canada.

The half-hour-long show premiered on July 21, 1996, and was hosted by Craig Kilborn until December 17, 1998. Jon Stewart then took over as the host from January 11, 1999 until August 6, 2015, making the show more strongly focused on politics and the national media, in contrast with the pop culture focus during Kilborn's tenure. Stewart was succeeded by Trevor Noah, whose tenure premiered on September 28, 2015. The Daily Show is the longest-running program on Comedy Central, and has won 23 Primetime Emmy Awards.

Describing itself as a fake news program, The Daily Show draws its comedy and satire from recent news stories, political figures, media organizations, and often uses self-referential humor as well. During Stewart's tenure, the show typically opened with a long monologue, relating to recent headlines and frequently featured exchanges with one or more Daily Show correspondents, who adopted absurd or humorously exaggerated takes on current events against Stewart's straight man persona. The final segment was devoted to a celebrity interview, with guests ranging from actors and musicians to nonfiction authors and political figures.

The program is popular among young audiences, with organizations such as the Pew Research Center suggesting that 74% of regular viewers are between 18 and 49, and that 10% of the audience watch the show for its news headlines, 2% for in-depth reporting, and 43% for entertainment, compared with 64% who watch CNN for the news headlines. Critics have chastised Stewart for not conducting sufficiently hard-hitting interviews with his political guests, some of whom he may have lampooned in previous segments. Stewart and other Daily Show writers have responded to such criticism by saying that they do not have any journalistic responsibility and that as comedians their only duty is to provide entertainment. Stewart's appearance on the CNN show Crossfire picked up this debate, where he chastised the CNN production and hosts for not conducting informative and current interviews on a news network.

Format

Each episode begins with announcer Drew Birns announcing the date and the introduction, "From Comedy Central's World News Headquarters in New York, this is The Daily Show with Jon Stewart," later changing to reflect Trevor Noah as the new host. Previously, the introduction was "This is The Daily Show, the most important television program, ever." The host then opens the show with a monologue drawing from current news stories and issues. Previously, the show had divided its news commentary into sections known as "Headlines", "Other News", and "This Just In"; these titles were dropped from regular use on October 28, 2002 and were last used on March 6, 2003.

The monologue segment is often followed by a segment featuring an exchange with a correspondent—typically introduced as the show's "senior" specialist in the subject at hand—either at the anchor desk with the host or reporting from a false location in front of a greenscreen showing stock footage. Their stated areas of expertise vary depending on the news story that is being discussed, and can range from relatively general to absurdly specific. The cast of correspondents is quite diverse, and many often sarcastically portray extreme stereotypes of themselves to poke fun at a news story, such as "Senior Latino Correspondent" or "Senior Youth Correspondent". They typically present absurd or humorously exaggerated takes on current events against the host's straight man.

While correspondents stated to be reporting abroad are usually performing in-studio in front of a greenscreen background, on rare occasions, cast members have recorded pieces on location. For instance, during the week of August 20, 2007, the show aired a series of segments called "Operation Silent Thunder: The Daily Show in Iraq" in which correspondent Rob Riggle reported from Iraq. In August 2008, Riggle traveled to China for a series of segments titled "Rob Riggle: Chasing the Dragon", which focused on the 2008 Beijing Olympics. Additionally, Jason Jones traveled to Iran in early June 2009 to report on the Iranian elections, and John Oliver traveled to South Africa for the series of segments "Into Africa" to report on the 2010 FIFA World Cup. In March 2012, John Oliver traveled to Gabon, on the west African coast, to report on the Gabonese government's decision to donate $2 million to UNESCO after the United States cut its funding for UNESCO earlier that year.

Correspondent segments feature a rotating supporting cast, and involve the show's members traveling to different locations to file comedic reports on current news stories and conduct interviews with people related to the featured issue. Topics have varied widely; during the early years of the show they tended toward character-driven human interest stories such as Bigfoot enthusiasts. Since Stewart began hosting in 1999, the focus of the show has become more political and the field pieces have come to more closely reflect current issues and debates. Under Kilborn and the early years of Stewart, most interviewees were either unaware or not entirely aware of the comedic nature of The Daily Show. However, since the show began to gain popularity—particularly following its coverage of the 2000 and 2004 presidential elections—most of the subjects now interviewed are aware of the comedic element.

Some segments have recurred periodically, such as "Back in Black" with Lewis Black, "This Week in God" and "Are You Prepared?!?" with Samantha Bee, "Trendspotting" with Demetri Martin, "Wilmore-Oliver Investigates" with John Oliver and Larry Wilmore, "You're Welcome" and "Money Talks" with John Hodgman. Since the 2003 invasion of Iraq, a common segment of the show has been dubbed "Mess O' Potamia", focusing on the United States' policies in the Middle East, especially Iraq. Elections in the United States were a prominent focus in the show's "Indecision" coverage throughout Stewart's time as host. Since 2000, the show has gone on the road to record week-long specials from the cities hosting the Democratic and Republican National Conventions. For the 2006 U.S. midterm elections, a week of episodes was recorded in the contested state of Ohio. The "Indecision" coverage of the 2000, 2004, 2006, 2008, and 2010 elections all culminated in live Election Night specials. On March 1, 2011, Stewart aired the first installment of Indecision 2012.

With Noah as host, one new recurring segment has been "What the Actual Fact", with correspondent Desi Lydic examining statements made by political figures during speeches or events. Under Noah, The continuation of Democalypse 2016 also took place with live shows after the Republican

National Convention and Democratic National Convention. It also went live for all three U.S presidential debates.

In the show's third act, the host conducts an interview with a celebrity guest. Guests come from a wide range of cultural sources, and include actors, musicians, authors, athletes, pundits and political figures. Since Stewart became host, the show's guest list has tended away from celebrities and more towards non-fiction authors and political pundits, as well as many prominent elected officials. While in the show's earlier years it struggled to book high-profile politicians—in 1999, for an Indecision 2000 segment, Steve Carell struggled to talk his way off Republican candidate John McCain's press overflow bus and onto the Straight Talk Express—it has since risen in popularity, particularly following the show's coverage of the 2000 and 2004 elections. In 2006, Rolling Stone described The Daily Show under Stewart as "the hot destination for anyone who wants to sell books or seem hip, from presidential candidates to military dictators", while Newsweek calls it "the coolest pit stop on television".

Prominent political guests have included U.S. President Barack Obama, Vice President Joe Biden, former Presidents Jimmy Carter and Bill Clinton, former British Prime Ministers Tony Blair and Gordon Brown, former Pakistani President Pervez Musharraf, Liberian President Ellen Johnson Sirleaf, Bolivian President Evo Morales, Jordanian King Abdullah II, Estonia Prime Minister Taavi Roivas and former Mexican President Vicente Fox. The show has played host to former and current members of the Administration and Cabinet as well as members of Congress. Numerous presidential candidates have appeared on the show during their campaigns, including John McCain, John Kerry and Barack Obama.

In a closing segment, there is a brief segue to the closing credits in the form of the host introducing "Your Moment of Zen", a humorous piece of video footage without commentary that has been part of the show's wrap-up since the series began in 1996. The segment often relates to a story covered earlier in the episode, but occasionally is merely a humorous or ridiculous clip. Occasionally, the segment is used as a tribute to someone who has died.

In October 2005, following The Colbert Report's premiere, a new feature was added to the closing segment in which Stewart would have a short exchange with "our good friend, Stephen Colbert at The Colbert Report", which aired immediately after. The two would have a scripted comedic exchange via split-screen from their respective sets. In 2007, the "toss" was cut back to twice per week, and by 2009 was once a week before gradually being phased out. It was used on the 2014 mid-term election night and again just before the final episode of The Colbert Report on December 18, 2014, and returned upon the premiere of The Nightly Show with Larry Wilmore. Stewart then regularly tossed to Wilmore at the end of his Monday night episodes.

Studio

The host sits at his desk on the elevated island stage in the style of a traditional news show. The show relocated from its original New York studio in late-1998 to NEP Studio 54 in New York City's Hell's Kitchen neighborhood, where it remained until 2005, when the studio was claimed by The Colbert Report. On July 11, 2005, the show premiered in its new studio, NEP Studio 52, at 733 11th Avenue, a few blocks west of its former location. The set of the new studio was given a sleeker, more formal look, including a backdrop of three large projection screens. The traditional guests' couch, which had been a part of the set since the show's premiere, was done away with in favor of simple upright chairs. The change was initially not well-received, spawning a backlash among some fans and prompting a "Bring Back the Couch" campaign. The campaign was mentioned on subsequent shows by Stewart and supported by Daily Show contributor Bob Wiltfong. The couch was eventually featured in a sweepstakes in which the winner received the couch, round-trip tickets to New York, tickets to the show, and a small sum of money.

On April 9, 2007 the show debuted a new set. The projection screens were revamped , a large, global map directly behind Stewart, a more open studio floor, and a J-shaped desk supported at one end by a globe. The intro was also updated; the graphics, display names, dates, and logos were all changed.

Production

The show's writers begin each day with a morning meeting where they review material that researchers have gathered from major newspapers, the Associated Press, cable news television channels and websites, and discuss headline material for the lead news segment. Throughout the morning they work on writing deadline pieces inspired by recent news, as well as longer-term projects. By lunchtime, Stewart—who describes his role as that of a managing editor—has begun to review headline jokes. The script is submitted by 3 pm, and at 4:15 there is a rehearsal. An hour is left for rewrites before a 6 pm taping in front of a live studio audience. While the studio capacity is limited, tickets to attend tapings are free and can be obtained if requested far enough in advance.

The Daily Show typically tapes four new episodes a week, Monday through Thursday, forty-two weeks a year. The show is broadcast at 11 PM Eastern/10 PM Central, a time when local television stations show their news reports and about half an hour before most other late-night comedy programs begin to go on the air. The program is rerun several times the next day, including a 7:30 PM Eastern/6:30 PM Central prime time broadcast.

History

The Daily Show was created by Lizz Winstead and Madeleine Smithberg and premiered on Comedy Central on July 22, 1996, having been marketed as a replacement for Politically Incorrect. Aiming to parody conventional newscasts, it featured a comedic monologue of the day's headlines from anchor Craig Kilborn, as well as mockumentary style on-location reports, in-studio segments and debates from regular correspondents Winstead, Brian Unger, Beth Littleford, and A. Whitney Brown.

Common segments included "This Day in Hasselhoff History" and "Last Weekend's Top-Grossing Films, Converted into Lira", in parody of entertainment news shows and their tendency to lead out to commercials with trivia such as celebrity birthdays. Another commercial lead-out featured Winstead's parents, on her answering machine, reading that day's "Final Jeopardy!" question and answer. In each show, Kilborn would conduct celebrity interviews, ending with a segment called "Five Questions" in which the guest was made to answer a series of questions that were typically a combination of obscure fact and subjective opinion. These are highlighted in a 1998 book titled The Daily Show: Five Questions, which contains transcripts of Kilborn's best interviews. Each episode concluded with a segment called "Your Moment of Zen" that showed random video clips of humorous and sometimes morbid interest such as visitors at a Chinese zoo feeding baby chickens to the alligators. Originally the show was recorded without a studio audience, featuring only the laughter of its own off-camera staff members. A studio audience was incorporated into the show for its second season, and has remained since.

The show was much less politically focused than it later became under Jon Stewart, having what Stephen Colbert described as a local news feel and involving more character-driven humor as opposed to news-driven humor. Winstead recalls that when the show was first launched there was constant debate regarding what the show's focus should be. While she wanted a more news-driven focus, the network was concerned that this would not appeal to viewers and pushed for "a little more of a hybrid of entertainment and politics". The show was slammed by some reviewers as being too mean-spirited, particularly towards the interview subjects of field pieces; a criticism acknowledged by some of the show's cast. Describing his time as a correspondent under Kilborn, Colbert says, "You wanted to take your soul off, put it on a wire hanger, and leave it in the closet before you got on the plane to do one of these pieces." One reviewer from The New York Times criticized the show for being too cruel and for lacking a central editorial vision or ideology, describing it as "bereft of an ideological or artistic center... precocious but empty."

There were reports of backstage friction between Kilborn and some of the female staff, particularly the show's co-creator Lizz Winstead. Winstead had not been involved in the hiring of Kilborn, and disagreed with him over what direction the show should take. "I spent eight months developing and staffing a show and seeking a tone with producers and writers. Somebody else put him in place. There were bound to be problems. I viewed the show as content-driven; he viewed it as host-driven," she said. In a 1997 Esquire magazine interview, Kilborn made a sexually explicit joke about Winstead. Comedy Central responded by suspending Kilborn without pay for one week, and Winstead quit soon after.

In 1998, Kilborn left The Daily Show in order to replace Tom Snyder on CBS's The Late Late Show. He claimed the "Five Questions" interview segment as intellectual property, disallowing any future Daily Show hosts from using it in their interviews. Correspondents Brian Unger and A. Whitney Brown left the show shortly before him, but the majority of the show's crew and writing staff stayed on. Kilborn's last show as host aired on December 17, 1998, ending a 386 episode tenure. Reruns were shown until Jon Stewart's debut four weeks later. Kilborn made a short appearance on Jon Stewart's final edition of the Daily Show saying "I knew you were going to run this thing into the ground."

Comedian Jon Stewart took over as host of the show, which was retitled The Daily Show with Jon Stewart, on January 11, 1999. Stewart had previously hosted Short Attention Span Theater on Comedy Central, two shows on MTV, as well as a syndicated late-night talk show, and had been cast in films and television. In taking over hosting from Kilborn, Stewart retained much of the same staff and on-air talent, allowing many pieces to transition without much trouble, while other features like "God Stuff", with John Bloom presenting an assortment of actual clips from various televangelists, and "Backfire", an in-studio debate between Brian Unger and A. Whitney Brown, evolved into the similar pieces of "This Week in God" and Stephen Colbert and Steve Carell's "Even Stevphen". Since the change, a number of new features have been, and continue to be, developed. The ending segment "Your Moment of Zen", previously consisting of a random selection of humorous videos, was diversified to sometimes include recaps or extended versions of news clips shown earlier in the show. The show's theme music, "Dog on Fire" by Bob

Mould, was re-recorded by They Might Be Giants shortly after Stewart joined the show.

Stewart served not only as host but also as a writer and executive producer of the series. Instrumental in shaping the voice of the show under Stewart was former editor of The Onion Ben Karlin who, along with fellow Onion contributor David Javerbaum, joined the staff in 1999 as head writer and was later promoted to executive producer. Their experience in writing for the satirical newspaper, which uses fake stories to mock real print journalism and current events, would influence the comedic direction of the show; Stewart recalls the hiring of Karlin as the point at which things " to take shape". Describing his approach to the show, Karlin said, "The main thing, for me, is seeing hypocrisy. People who know better saying things that you know they don't believe."

Under Stewart and Karlin The Daily Show developed a markedly different style, bringing a sharper political focus to the humor than the show previously exhibited. Then-correspondent Stephen Colbert recalls that Stewart specifically asked him to have a political viewpoint, and to allow his passion for issues to carry through into his comedy. Colbert says that whereas under Kilborn the focus was on "human interest-y" pieces, with Stewart as host the show's content became more "issues and news driven", particularly after the beginning of the 2000 election campaign with which the show dealt in its "Indecision 2000" coverage. Stewart himself describes the show's coverage of the 2000 election recount as the point at which the show found its editorial voice. "That's when I think we tapped into the emotional angle of the news for us and found our editorial footing," he says. Following the September 11th attacks, The Daily Show went off the air for nine days. Upon its return, Stewart opened the show with a somber monologue, that, according to Jeremy Gillick and Nonna Gorilovskaya, addressed both the absurdity and importance of his role as a comedian. Commented Stewart:

Gillick and Gorilovskaya point to the September 11 attacks and the beginning of the wars in Afghanistan and Iraq as the point at which Jon Stewart emerged as a trusted national figure. Robert Thompson, the director of the Bleier Center for Television and Popular Culture at Syracuse University, recalled of this period, "When all the news guys were walking on eggshells, Jon was hammering those questions about WMDs."

During Stewart's tenure, the role of the correspondent has broadened to encompass not only field segments but also frequent in-studio exchanges. Under Kilborn, Colbert says that his work as a correspondent initially involved "character driven pieces—like, you know, guys who believe in Bigfoot." However, as the focus of the show has become more news-driven, correspondents have increasingly been used in studio pieces, either as experts discussing issues at the anchor desk or as field journalists reporting from false locations in front of a green screen. Colbert says that this change has allowed correspondents to be more involved with the show, as it has permitted them to work more closely with the host and writers.

The show's 2000 and 2004 election coverage, combined with a new satirical edge, helped to catapult Stewart and The Daily Show to new levels of popularity and critical respect. Since Stewart became host, the show has won 23 Primetime Emmy Awards and three Peabody Awards, and its ratings have steadily increased. In 2003, the show was averaging nearly a million viewers, an increase of nearly threefold since the show's inception as Comedy Central became available in more households. By September 2008, the show averaged nearly two million viewers per night. Senator Barack Obama's interview on October 29, 2008, pulled in 3.6 million viewers.

The move towards greater involvement in political issues and the increasing popularity of the show in certain key demographics have led to examinations of where the views of the show fit in the political spectrum. Adam Clymer, among many others, has argued that The Daily Show is more critical of Republicans than Democrats. Stewart, who voted Democratic in the 2004 presidential election, says that the show does have a more liberal point of view, but that it is not "a liberal organization" with a political agenda and its duty first and foremost is to be funny. He acknowledges that the show is not necessarily an "equal opportunity offender", explaining that Republicans tended to provide more comedic fodder because "I think we consider those with power and influence targets and those without it, not." In an interview in 2005, when asked how he responded to critics claiming that The Daily Show is overly liberal, Stephen Colbert, also a self-proclaimed Democrat, said in an interview during the Bush Administration, when the Republicans held a majority in the House and Senate: "We are liberal, but Jon's very respectful of the Republican guests, and, listen, if liberals were in power it would be easier to attack them, but Republicans have the executive, legislative and judicial branches, so making fun of Democrats is like kicking a child, so it's just not worth it."

Stewart is critical of Democratic politicians for being weak, timid, or ineffective. He said in an interview with Larry King, prior to the 2006 elections, "I honestly don't feel that make an impact. They have forty-nine percent of the vote and three percent of the power. At a certain point you go, 'Guys, pick up your game.'" He has targeted them for failing to effectively stand on some issues, such as the war in Iraq, describing them as "incompetent" and "unable... to locate their asses, even when presented with two hands and a special ass map."

Karlin, then the show's executive producer, said in a 2004 interview that while there is a collective sensibility among the staff which, "when filtered through Jon and the correspondents, feels uniform," the principal goal of the show is comedy. "If you have a legitimately funny joke in support of the notion that gay people are an affront to God, we'll put that motherfucker on!"

On November 17, 2009, Vice President Joe Biden appeared on the show, making him the first sitting vice president to do so. On October 27, 2010, President Barack Obama became the first sitting U.S. president to be interviewed on the show, wherein Obama commented he "loved" the show. Obama took issue with Stewart's suggestion that his health care program was "timid."

After the United States Senate failed to pass and the media failed to cover the James Zadroga 9/11 Health and Compensation Act, which would provide health monitoring and financial aid to sick first responders of the September 11 attacks, Stewart dedicated the entire December 16, 2010, broadcast to the issue. During the next week, a revived version of the bill gained new life, with the potential of being passed before the winter recess. Stewart was praised by both politicians and affected first responders for the bill's passage. According to Syracuse University professor of television, radio and film Robert J. Thompson, "Without him, it's unlikely it would've passed. I don't think Brian Williams, Katie Couric or Diane Sawyer would've been allowed to do this."

Due to the 2007–2008 Writers Guild of America strike, the show went on hiatus on November 5, 2007. Although the strike continued until February

2008, the show returned to air on January 7, 2008, without its staff of writers. In solidarity with the writers, the show was referred to as A Daily Show with Jon Stewart rather than The Daily Show with Jon Stewart, until the end of the strike. As a member of the Writers Guild of America, Stewart was barred from writing any material for the show himself which he or his writers would ordinarily write. As a result, Stewart and the correspondents largely ad-libbed the show around planned topics. In an effort to fill time while keeping to these restrictions, the show aired or re-aired some previously recorded segments, and Stewart engaged in a briefly recurring mock feud with fellow late-night hosts Stephen Colbert and Conan O'Brien. The strike officially ended on February 12, 2008, with the show's writers returning to work the following day, at which point the title of The Daily Show was restored.

Starting in June 2013 Jon Stewart took a twelve-week break to direct Rosewater, a drama about a journalist jailed by Iran for four months. John Oliver replaced Stewart at the anchor desk for two months, to be followed by one month of reruns. Oliver received positive reviews for his hosting, leading to his departure from the show in December 2013 for his own show Last Week Tonight with John Oliver, which debuted April 27, 2014 on HBO.

On February 10, 2015, Stewart announced that he would be leaving the show later in the year. Comedy Central indicated in a statement that The Daily Show would continue without Stewart, saying it would "endure for years to come".

On June 25, 2015, Comedy Central announced that to lead up to Stewart's final episode, it would hold "Your Month of Zen"—an online marathon streaming every episode of Stewart's tenure from June 26 to August 6, 2015.

On August 6, 2015, Stewart's final episode aired as an hour-long special in three segments. The first featured a reunion of a majority of the correspondents and contributors from throughout the show's history as well as a pre-recorded "anti-tribute" from various frequent guests and "friends" of the show. The second segment featured a pre-recorded tour of the Daily Show production facility and studio introducing all of the show's staff and crew. The final segment featured a short farewell speech from Stewart followed by the final "Moment of Zen" : a performance of "Land of Hope and Dreams" and "Born to Run" by Bruce Springsteen and the E Street Band.

On March 30, 2015, it was announced that Trevor Noah would replace Stewart as host of The Daily Show. Trevor Noah's first show was on September 28, 2015 with comedian Kevin Hart as his first guest. Noah's premiere episode was simulcast by Viacom on Comedy Central, Nick-at-Nite, Spike, MTV, MTV2, mtvU, VH1, VH1 Classic, BET, Centric, CMT, TV Land and Logo TV.

In addition to changes in the tone of the show, Noah has also implemented stylistic changes to the show, with an updated set, new graphics and his monologue often taking place while standing in front of a screen as opposed to sitting at the desk. Trevor also increased impersonations & characterisations in his comedy on the show, due to his ability to speak in multiple accents and five languages beside English.

The debut of The Daily Show with Trevor Noah also brought along three correspondents: Roy Wood Jr., Desi Lydic and Ronny Chieng.

In January 2016, The Daily Show with Trevor Noah started to use a modified version of the show's previous theme, composed by Timbaland and King Logan. The theme is a remix of the old theme with the addition of rock.

Trevor Noah also avoided talking too much about Fox News, as Stewart was previously known for. "The Daily Show was based on an emerging 24 hour news cycle, that's everything it was, that's what inspired The Daily Show. Now you look at news and it's changed. It's no longer predicated around 24 hour news. There are so many different choices. Half of it is online now. Now you've got the 'Gawker's, the 'Buzzfeed's. The way people are drawing their news is soundbites and headlines and click-bait links has changed everything. The biggest challenge is going to be an exciting one I'm sure is how are we going to bring all of that together looking at it from a bigger lens as opposed to just going after one source — which was historically Fox News" Noah said at a press conference before the shows debut.

On December 8, 2015, former host Jon Stewart returned to The Daily Show for the first time in an extended length show to return attention to extending the James Zadroga 9/11 Health and Compensation Act, otherwise referred to as 9/11 First Responders Bill, which Stewart explained had been blocked by Paul Ryan and Mitch McConnell for political reasons.

On October 20, 2016 and October 24, 2016, Trevor Noah was unable to host a scheduled taping of The Daily Show due to illness, correspondent Jordan Klepper guest hosted.

Correspondents, contributors, and staff

The show's correspondents have two principal roles: experts with satirical senior titles that Noah interviews about certain issues, or hosts of field reporting segments which often involve humorous commentary and interviews relating to a current issue. The current team of correspondents collectively known as "The Best F#@king News Team Ever" includes Ronny Chieng,

Jordan Klepper, Desi Lydic, Hasan Minhaj, and Roy Wood, Jr. Contributors appear on a less frequent basis, often with their own unique recurring segment or topic. Current contributors are Lewis Black, Kristen Schaal, John Hodgman, Michelle Wolf, Adam Lowitt and Eliza Cossio. Ben Karlin says that the on-air talent contribute in many ways to the material they perform, playing an integral role in the creation of their field pieces as well as being involved with their scripted studio segments, either taking part early on in the writing process or adding improvised material during the rehearsal.

The show has featured a number of well-known comedians throughout its run and is notable for boosting the careers of several of these. Scott Dikkers, editor-in-chief of The Onion, describes it as a key launching pad for comedic talent, saying that "I don't know if there's a better show you could put on your resume right now." Steve Carell, who was a correspondent between 1999 and 2005 before moving on to a movie career and starring television role in The Office, credits Stewart and The Daily Show with his success. In 2005, the show's longest-serving correspondent, Stephen Colbert, became the host of the spin-off The Colbert Report, earning critical and popular acclaim. Colbert would host the program until he was chosen to replace David Letterman as host of CBS's Late Show in 2015. Ed Helms, a former correspondent from 2002 to 2006, also starred on NBC's The Office and was a main character in the 2009 hit The Hangover. After filling in as host during Stewart's two-month absence in 2014, John Oliver went on to host his own show on HBO, Last Week Tonight with John Oliver. In 2016, former correspondent Samantha Bee launched her own late-night talk show Full Frontal with Samantha Bee. Jason Jones, another former correspondent, serves as executive producer for the show.

In June 2010, actress-comedian Olivia Munn began a tryout period on the show as a correspondent. Her credentials were questioned by Irin Carmon of the website Jezebel, who suggested that Munn was better known as a sex symbol than as a comedian. Carmon's column was denounced by Munn and the Daily Show's female writers, producers, and correspondents, 32 of whom posted a rebuttal on the show's website in which they asserted that the description of the Daily Show office given by the Jezebel piece was not accurate. Munn appeared as a Daily Show correspondent in a total of 16 episodes, from June 2010 to September 2011.

Wyatt Cenac had a tumultuous tenure on the show, revealing in a July 2015 interview on WTF with Marc Maron, that his departure stemmed in part from a heated argument he had with Jon Stewart in June 2011 over a bit about Republican Presidential candidate Herman Cain. However, Cenac did return for Stewart's final episode to bid him farewell and the two exchanged an intentionally awkward conversation.

Reception

Television ratings from 2008 show that the program generally drew 1.45 to 1.6 million viewers nightly, a high figure for cable television. By the end of 2013 The Daily Show's ratings hit 2.5 million viewers nightly. In demographic terms, the viewership is skewed to a relatively young and well-educated audience compared to traditional news shows. A 2004 Nielsen Media Research study commissioned by Comedy Central put the median age at 35. During the 2004 U.S. presidential election, the show received more male viewers in the 18- to 34-year-old age demographic than Nightline, Meet the Press, Hannity & Colmes and all of the evening news broadcasts. Because of this, commentators such as Howard Dean and Ted Koppel posit that Stewart serves as a real source of news for young people, regardless of his intentions.

The show's writers reject the idea that The Daily Show has become a source of news for young people. Stewart argues that Americans are living in an "age of information osmosis" in which it is close to impossible to gain one's news from any single source, and says that his show succeeds comedically because the viewers already have some knowledge about current events. "Our show would not be valuable to people who didn't understand the news because it wouldn't make sense," he argues. "We make assumptions about your level of knowledge that... if we were your only source of news, you would just watch our show and think, 'I don't know what's happening.'"

A 2006 study published by Indiana University tried to compare the substantive amount of information of The Daily Show against prime time network news broadcasts, and concluded that when it comes to substance, there is little difference between The Daily Show and other news outlets. The study contended that, since both programs are more focused on the nature of "infotainment" and ratings than on the dissemination of information, both are broadly equal in terms of the amount of substantial news coverage they offer.

As the lines between comedy show and news show have blurred, Jon Stewart has come under pressure in some circles to engage in more serious journalism. Tucker Carlson and Daily Show co-creator Lizz Winstead have chastised Stewart for criticizing politicians and newspeople in his solo segments and then, in interviews with the same people, rarely taking them to task face-to-face. In 2004, Winstead expressed a desire for Stewart to ask harder satirical questions, saying, "When you are interviewing a Richard Perle or a Kissinger, if you give them a pass, then you become what you are satirizing. You have a war criminal sitting on your couch—to just let him be a war criminal sitting on your couch means you are having to respect some kind of boundary." She has argued that The Daily Show's success and access to the youth vote should allow Stewart to press political guests harder without fearing that they will not return to the show. In 2010, Winstead had changed her views, commenting that since 2004, Stewart did some of the hardest-hitting interviews on TV. Stewart said in 2003 that he does not think of himself as a social or media critic and rejects the idea that he has any journalistic role as an interviewer.

During Stewart's appearance on CNN's Crossfire, Stewart criticized that show and said that it was "hurting America" by sensationalizing debates and enabling political spin. When co-host Carlson argued that Stewart himself had not asked John Kerry substantial questions when Kerry appeared on The Daily Show, Stewart countered that it was not his job to give hard-hitting interviews and that a "fake news" comedy program should not be held to the same standards as real journalism. "You're on CNN!" Stewart said, "The show that leads into me is puppets making crank phone calls! What is wrong with you?" Media critic Dan Kennedy says that Stewart came off as disingenuous in this exchange because "you can't interview Bill Clinton, Richard Clarke, Bill O'Reilly, Bob Dole, etc., etc., and still say you're just a comedian."

A 2004 study into the effect of The Daily Show on viewers' attitudes found that participants had a more negative opinion of both President Bush and then Democratic presidential nominee John Kerry. Participants also expressed more cynical views of the electoral system and news media. Political scientists Jody Baumgartner and Jonathan Morris, who conducted the study, state that it is not clear how such cynicism would affect the political behavior of the show's viewers. While disillusionment and negative perceptions of the presidential candidates could discourage watchers from voting, Baumgartner and Morris say it is also possible that discontent could prompt greater involvement and that by following the show, viewers may potentially become more engaged and informed voters, with a broader political knowledge.

Rachel Larris, who has also conducted an academic study of The Daily Show, disputes the findings of Baumgartner and Morris. Larris argues that the study measured cynicism in overly broad terms, and that it would be extremely hard to find a causal link between viewing The Daily Show and thinking or acting in a particular way. Bloggers such as Marty Kaplan of The Huffington Post argue that so long as Stewart's comedy is grounded in truth, responsibility for increased cynicism belongs to the political and media figures themselves, not the comedian who satirizes them.

Stewart himself says that he does not perceive his show as cynical. "It's so interesting to me that people talk about late-night comedy being cynical," he says. "What's more cynical than forming an ideological news network like Fox and calling it 'fair and balanced'? What we do, I almost think, is adorable in its idealism." Stewart has said that he does not take any joy in the failings of American government, despite the comedic fodder they provide. "We're not the guys at the craps table betting against the line," he said on Larry King Live. "If government suddenly became inspiring... we would be the happiest people in the world to turn our attention to idiots like, you know, media people, no offense."

In July 2009, Time magazine held an online poll entitled "Now that Walter Cronkite has passed on, who is America's most trusted newscaster?" Jon Stewart won with 44% of the vote, 15 points ahead of Brian Williams in second place with 29%. Stewart downplayed the results on the show stating "It was an Internet poll and I was the 'None of the above' option".

In December 2013, TV Guide ranked Jon Stewart's run on the show at #53 on its list of the 60 Best Series of All Time.

In late 2004, the National Annenberg Election Survey at the University of Pennsylvania ran a study of American television viewers and found that fans of The Daily Show had a more accurate idea of the facts behind the 2004 presidential election than most others, including those who primarily got their news through the national network evening newscasts and through reading newspapers. However, in a 2004 campaign survey conducted by the Pew Research Center those who cited comedy shows such as The Daily Show as a source for news were among the least informed on campaign events and key aspects of the candidates' backgrounds while those who cited the Internet, National Public Radio, and news magazines were the most informed. Even when age and education were taken into account, the people who learned about the campaigns through the Internet were still found to be the most informed, while those who learned from comedy shows were the least informed.

In a survey released by the Pew Research Center in April 2007, viewers who watch both The Colbert Report and The Daily Show tend to be more knowledgeable about news than audiences of other news sources. Approximately 54% of The Colbert Report and The Daily Show viewers scored in the high knowledge range, followed by Jim Lehrer's program at 53% and Bill O'Reilly's program at 51%, significantly higher than the 34% of network morning show viewers. The survey shows that changing news formats have not made much difference on how much the public knows about national and international affairs, but adds that there is no clear connection between news formats and what audiences know. The Project for Excellence in Journalism released a content analysis report suggesting that The Daily Show comes close to providing the complete daily news.

Awards and nominations

Under host Jon Stewart, The Daily Show rose to critical acclaim. It has received two Peabody Awards for its coverage of the 2000 and 2004 presidential elections. Between 2001 and 2015, it has been awarded 21 Primetime Emmy Awards in the categories of Outstanding Variety, Music, or Comedy Series and Outstanding Writing for a Variety, Music, or Comedy Program, and a further seven nominations. The show has also been honored by GLAAD, the Television Critics Association, and the Satellite Awards. America : A Citizen's Guide to Democracy Inaction, the 2004 bestseller written by Stewart and the writing staff of The Daily Show, was recognized by Publishers Weekly as its "Book of the Year", and its abridged audiobook edition received the 2005 Grammy Award for Best Comedy Album. In September 2010, Time magazine selected the series as one of "The 100 Best TV Shows of All-TIME".

Global editions

The Daily Show airs on various networks worldwide; in addition, an edited version of the show called The Daily Show: Global Edition is produced each week specifically for overseas audiences. It has been airing outside of the U.S. on CNN International and other overseas networks since September 2002. This edition runs for half an hour and contains a selection of segments including one guest interview from the preceding week's shows, usually from the Monday or Tuesday episode. Stewart provides an exclusive introductory monologue in front of an audience, usually about the week's prevalent international news story, and closing comments without an audience present. When aired on CNN International, the broadcast is prefaced by a written disclaimer: "The show you are about to watch is a news parody. Its stories are not fact checked. Its reporters are not journalists. And its opinions are not fully thought through."

Between 2001 and 2006, Westwood One broadcast small, ninety-second portions of the show to various radio stations across America.

In Canada, The Daily Show is aired on The Comedy Network, in simulcast with the Comedy Central airing, as well as on the CTV broadcast network at 12:05 a.m. local time, following late local newscasts.

In the United Kingdom and Ireland, the digital television channel More4 used to broadcast episodes of The Daily Show Tuesday through Friday evenings with the Global Edition, which is uncensored, airs on Mondays; regular episodes air the evening following their U.S. airing. More4 was the first international broadcaster to syndicate entire Daily Show episodes, though they made edits to the program due to content, language, length or commercial references. The program was also available to watch via the internet video on demand service 4oD. However, the 'toss' to The Colbert Report was usually included even though it was aired on FX, another channel. In addition, the placement of commercial breaks followed the UK format, with one break midway through the show rather than several short breaks at various points. When The Daily Show was on hiatus, either re-runs or alternative content were aired. Since January 2011, only the Global Edition is broadcast. In July 2012 Comedy Central announced that The Daily Show would be shown on Comedy Central Extra in the same format as previously on More4, with episodes shown 24 hours after airing in the U.S. The show aired on the channel from July 2012 to April 2015.

The Global Edition of the week of July 20, 2011 was not aired in the UK as it included a segment mocking Rupert Murdoch's appearance before the House of Commons Culture, Media and Sport Committee in relation to the News International phone hacking scandal. Parliamentary rules ban parliamentary proceedings from being broadcast in a satirical context. Stewart dedicated a segment of the show on August 2, 2011 to lampooning the censorship of the episode in Britain. In May that year, The Daily Show mocked the ban on using footage of the Royal Wedding in a satirical context with an animated video that showed Paddington Bear, Gollum and Adolf Hitler as guests at the wedding, and depicted its attendants engaging in various forms of violent and sexual behavior. Stewart later discussed the ban with guest Keira Knightley.

The Daily Show is aired in India on Comedy Central India.

The Daily Show is aired on Australian Pay TV channel, The Comedy Channel, weeknights at 6:30pm. Free-to-air digital channel ABC2 began broadcasting the show without commercial breaks in March 2010, but discontinued in January 2011 when The Comedy Channel obtained exclusive rights; episodes were also available on the network's online service ABC iView shortly after airing. The Comedy Channel air the show together with The Colbert Report, and both air the Global Edition on Mondays and the regular edition Tuesday through Friday. The Global Edition was previously shown weekend late nights on SBS before moving to Network TEN.

In Portugal, it airs with no commercial breaks.

In North Africa and the Middle East, the Daily Show has been broadcast since 2008 on Showtime Arabia. The regular as well as the Global Edition episodes can currently be seen on OSN First HD, which also broadcasts The Colbert

Report. However episodes are often edited if they contain topics deemed inappropriate for the region.

Episodes of the U.S. version are also available online the next day at Comedy Central's official Daily Show website, although this service is not available in all countries. However, clips for UK and Ireland viewers became available on the UK Comedy Central website in December 2011.

Spin-offs

A spin-off, The Colbert Report, was announced in early May 2005. The show starred former correspondent Stephen Colbert, and served as Comedy Central's answer to the programs of media pundits such as Bill O'Reilly. Colbert, Stewart, and Ben Karlin developed the idea for the show based on a series of faux television commercials that had been created for an earlier Daily Show segment. They pitched the concept to Comedy Central chief Doug Herzog, who agreed to run the show for eight weeks without first creating a pilot. The Colbert Report premiered on October 17, 2005 and aired following The Daily Show for nine years. Initial ratings satisfied Comedy Central and less than three weeks after its debut the show was renewed for a year. The Colbert Report was produced by Jon Stewart's production company, Busboy Productions.

In 2014 it was announced that Colbert would leave Comedy Central to host The Late Show with Stephen Colbert on CBS in 2015, following the retirement of David Letterman. The final episode of The Colbert Report aired on December 18, 2014.

On May 9, 2014 it was announced that Larry Wilmore had been selected to host a show on Comedy Central to serve as a replacement for The Colbert Report. On January 19, 2015 Wilmore began hosting The Nightly Show with

Larry Wilmore, a late-night panel talk show. It was produced by Busboy Productions. On August 15, 2016, Comedy Central announced that Wilmore's show had been cancelled. The show ended on August 18, 2016, with a total of 259 episodes.

A local spin-off of the show called The Daily Show: Nederlandse Editie premiered on the Dutch Comedy Central on January 31, 2011. The program is similar to the original, except with Dutch news and a Dutch view on international news. The show is hosted by comedian Jan-Jaap van der Wal, who was a team captain on Dit was het nieuws, the Dutch edition of Have I Got News For You. The first episode featured a guest appearance by Jon Stewart , who gave his official blessing for the show. This is also the first and still only franchise of The Daily Show. The 'Dutch Edition' didn't make it past the test run of 12 episodes due to lack of viewers.

Unofficial spin-offs

The Daily Show's satirical format has inspired international versions unaffiliated with Comedy Central.

Jon Stewart is an American comedian, writer, producer, director, actor, media critic, and former television host. He was the host of The Daily Show, a satirical news program on Comedy Central, from 1999 until 2015.

Stewart started as a stand-up comedian, but branched into television as host of Short Attention Span Theater for Comedy Central. He went on to host his own show on MTV, The Jon Stewart Show, and then hosted You Wrote It, You Watch It, also on MTV. He has also had several film roles as an actor, but has done few cinematic projects since becoming the host of The Daily Show in 1999. He was also a writer and co-executive producer of the show. After

Stewart joined, The Daily Show steadily gained popularity and critical acclaim, and his work won 22 Primetime Emmy Awards.

Stewart has gained acclaim as an acerbic, satirical critic of personality-driven media shows, in particular those of the U.S. media networks such as CNN, Fox News, and MSNBC. Critics say Stewart benefits from a double standard: he critiques other news shows from the safe, removed position of his "fake news" desk. Stewart agrees, saying that neither his show nor his channel purports to be anything other than satire and comedy. In spite of its self-professed entertainment mandate, The Daily Show has been nominated for news and journalism awards. Stewart hosted the 78th and 80th Academy Awards. He is the co-author of America : A Citizen's Guide to Democracy Inaction, which was one of the best-selling books in the U.S. in 2004, and Earth : A Visitor's Guide to the Human Race, released in 2010.

Stewart announced on February 10, 2015, during a taping of The Daily Show, that he would leave the show before the end of 2015, but assured fans that he was not retiring and suggested that he would continue writing and may return to stand-up comedy or as a part-time correspondent. Stewart's final show aired on August 6, 2015.

Early life

Jon Stewart was born Jonathan Stuart Leibowitz on November 28, 1962, in New York City, to Marian , a teacher and later educational consultant, and Donald Leibowitz , a professor of physics at The College of New Jersey and Thomas Edison State College. Stewart's family is Jewish, and emigrated to the U.S. from Poland, Ukraine and Belarus ; one of his grandfathers was born in

Manzhouli. Stewart is the second of four sons, with older brother Lawrence and younger brothers Dan and Matthew.

Stewart's parents divorced when Stewart was eleven years old, and Stewart was apparently largely estranged from his father. Because of his strained relationship with his father, which in 2015 he described as "still 'complicated'", he dropped his surname and began using his middle name, Stuart. Stewart stated, "There was a thought of using my mother's maiden name, but I thought that would be just too big a fuck you to my dad...Did I have some problems with my father? Yes. Yet people always view through the prism of ethnic identity." He had his surname legally changed to Stewart in 2001. Stewart and his brother Lawrence, who was previously the Chief Operating Officer of NYSE Euronext, grew up in Lawrenceville, New Jersey, where they attended Lawrence High School. According to Stewart, he was subjected to anti-Semitic bullying as a child. He describes himself in high school as "very into Eugene Debs and a bit of a leftist."

Stewart grew up in the era of the Vietnam War and the Watergate scandal, which inspired in him "a healthy skepticism towards official reports". His first job was working at a Woolworths at which his brother Lawrence worked, and jokingly describes being fired by Lawrence as one of the "scarring events" of his youth.

Stewart graduated in 1984 from the College of William & Mary in Virginia, where he played on the soccer team and initially majored in chemistry before switching to psychology. While at William & Mary, Stewart became a brother of the Pi Kappa Alpha Fraternity, but later disassociated himself from the fraternity and left after six months. "My college career was waking up late, memorizing someone else's notes, doing bong hits, and going to soccer practice," he would later recall. His soccer coach would later describe him as a "good player" with "high energy". After college, Stewart held numerous jobs: a contingency planner for the New Jersey Department of Human Services, a contract administrator for the City University of New York, a puppeteer for children with disabilities, a soccer coach at Gloucester High School in Virginia, a caterer, a busboy, a shelf stocker at Woolworth's, a bartender at the Franklin Corner Tavern , and a bartender at the legendary City Gardens in Trenton, New Jersey. He has said that working at City Gardens was a pivotal moment for him: "finding this place City Gardens was like, 'Oh, maybe I'm not a giant weirdo. Maybe there are other people who have a similar sense of yearning for something other than what they have now.' I think it inspired a lot of people, man. It was a very creative environment. It was a place of great possibility."

Career

With a reputation for being a funny man in school, Jon Stewart returned to New York City in 1986 to try his hand at the comedy club circuit, but he could not muster the courage to get on stage until the following year. He made his stand-up debut at The Bitter End, where his comedic idol, Woody Allen, also began. He began using the stage name "Jon Stewart" by dropping his last name and changing the spelling of his middle name "Stuart" to "Stewart". He often jokes this is because people had difficulty with the pronunciation of Leibowitz or it "sounded too Hollywood" . He has implied that the name change was actually due to a strained relationship with his father, with whom Stewart no longer had any contact.

Stewart became a regular at the Comedy Cellar, where he was the last performer every night. For two years, he would perform at 2 a.m. while developing his comedic style. In 1989, Stewart landed his first television job as a writer for Caroline's Comedy Hour. In 1991, he began co-hosting Comedy Central's Short Attention Span Theater, with Patty Rosborough. In 1992, Stewart hosted the short-lived You Wrote It, You Watch It on MTV, which invited viewers to send in their stories to be acted out by the comedy troupe, The State.

Stewart felt his career did not take off until a March 1993 appearance on NBC's Late Night with David Letterman. He was considered a finalist to take over Letterman's position upon his departure from the program, but it was instead given to relatively unknown Conan O'Brien.

Later in 1993, Stewart developed The Jon Stewart Show, a talk show on MTV. The Jon Stewart Show was the first talk show on that network and was an instant hit, becoming the second-highest rated MTV show behind Beavis and Butt-head. In 1994, Paramount canceled The Arsenio Hall Show and, with new corporate sibling MTV , launched an hour-long syndicated late-night version of The Jon Stewart Show. Many local affiliates had moved Hall's show to 2 a.m. during its decline and Stewart's show inherited such early morning time slots in many cities. Ratings were dismal and the show was canceled in June 1995.

Among the fans of the show was David Letterman, who was the final guest of The Jon Stewart Show. Letterman signed Stewart with his production company, Worldwide Pants. Stewart then became a frequent guest host for Tom Snyder on The Late Late Show with Tom Snyder, which was produced by Letterman and aired after the Late Show on CBS. This led to much speculation that Stewart would soon replace Snyder permanently, but Stewart was instead offered the time slot after Snyder's, which he turned down.

In 1996 Stewart hosted a short-lived talk show called "Where's Elvis This Week?" It was a half-hour, weekly comedy television program that aired on Sunday nights in the United Kingdom on BBC Two. It was filmed at the CBS Broadcast Center in New York City and featured a set of panelists, two from the United Kingdom and two from the United States, who discussed news items and cultural issues. The show premiered in the UK on October 6, 1996; five episodes aired in total. Notable panelists included Dave Chappelle, Eddie Izzard, Phil Jupitus, Nora Ephron, Craig Kilborn, Christopher Hitchens, Armando Iannucci, Norm Macdonald, and Helen Gurley Brown. In 1997, Stewart was chosen as the host and interviewer for George Carlin's 10th HBO special, 40 years of Comedy.

In 1999, Stewart began hosting The Daily Show on Comedy Central when Craig Kilborn left the show to replace Tom Snyder on The Late Late Show. The show blends humor with the day's top news stories, usually in politics, while simultaneously poking fun at politicians and many newsmakers as well as the news media itself. In an interview on The O'Reilly Factor, Stewart denied the show has any intentional political agenda, saying the goal was "schnicks and giggles." "The same weakness that drove me into comedy also informs my show," meaning that he was uncomfortable talking without hearing the audience laugh. "Stewart does not offer us cynicism for its own sake, but as a playful way to offer the kinds of insights that are not permitted in more serious news formats that slavishly cling to official account of events."

Stewart has since hosted almost all airings of the program, except for a few occasions when correspondents such as Stephen Colbert, Rob Corddry, Jason Jones and Steve Carell subbed for him, and during John Oliver's stint as host during the summer of 2013. Stewart has won a total of twenty Primetime

Emmy Awards for The Daily Show as either a writer or producer, and two for producing The Colbert Report, winning a total of twenty-two Primetime Emmy Awards, having the most wins for a male individual. In 2005, Stewart and The Daily Show received the Grammy Award for Best Comedy Album for the audio book edition of America : A Citizen's Guide to Democracy Inaction. In 2000 and 2004, the show won two Peabody Awards for its coverage of the presidential elections relevant to those years, called "Indecision 2000" and "Indecision 2004", respectively.

The show of September 20, 2001, the first show after the attacks of September 11, 2001, began with no introduction. Before this, the introduction included footage of a fly-in towards the World Trade Center and New York City. The first nine minutes of the show included a tearful Stewart discussing his personal view on the event. His remarks ended as follows:

In mid-2002, amid rumors that David Letterman was going to switch from CBS to ABC when his contract ran out, Stewart was rumored as Letterman's replacement on CBS. Ultimately, Letterman renewed his contract with CBS. On the March 9, 2002, episode of Saturday Night Live, hosted by Stewart, a "Weekend Update" sketch poked fun at the situation.

In late 2002, ABC offered Stewart his own talk show to air right before Nightline. Stewart's contract with The Daily Show was near expiring, and he expressed strong interest. ABC, however, decided to give another Comedy Central figure, Jimmy Kimmel, the pre-Nightline slot.

On April 4, 2006, Stewart confronted U.S. Senator John McCain about his decision to appear at Liberty University, an institution founded by Jerry Falwell, whom McCain had previously denounced as one of the "agents of intolerance". In the interchange, Stewart asked McCain, "You're not freaking out on us? Are you freaking out on us, because if you're freaking out and you're going into the crazy base world—are you going into crazy base world?" McCain replied, "I'm afraid so." The clip was played on CNN and created a surge of articles across the blogosphere.

In 2007, The Daily Show was involved in former correspondent Stephen Colbert's announcement that he would run for president in 2008. In 2008, Stewart appeared on the news program Democracy Now! A 2008 New York Times story questioned whether he was, in a phrase originally used to describe longtime network news anchor Walter Cronkite, "the most trusted man in America".

On April 28, 2009, during a discussion on torture with Clifford May, Stewart expressed his opinion that former President Harry S. Truman was a war criminal for his use of the atomic bomb on Japan during World War II. Moments later, Stewart defended his assertion: "Here's what I think of the atom bombs. I think if you dropped an atom bomb fifteen miles offshore and you said, 'The next one's coming and hitting you', then I would think it's okay. To drop it on a city, and kill a hundred thousand people. Yeah. I think that's criminal." On April 30, 2009, Stewart apologized on his program, and stated he did not believe Truman was a war criminal: "I shouldn't have said that, and I did. So I say right now, no, I don't believe that to be the case. The atomic bomb, a very complicated decision in the context of a horrific war, and I walk that back because it was in my estimation a stupid thing to say."

In April 2010, Comedy Central renewed Stewart's contract to host The Daily Show into 2013. According to the Forbes list of Celebrities in 2008, he was earning $14 million a year.

On September 16, 2010, Stewart and Stephen Colbert announced a rally for October 30, known as the Rally to Restore Sanity and/or Fear. It took place on the National Mall in Washington, D.C. and attracted an estimated 215,000 participants. In December 2010, Stewart was credited by the White House and other media and political news outlets for bringing awareness of the Republican filibuster on the James Zadroga 9/11 Health and Compensation Act to the public, leading to the ultimate passing of the bill which provides health benefits to first responders whose health has been adversely affected by their work at Ground Zero.

On the show of January 10, 2011, Stewart began with a monologue about the shootings in Tucson, AZ. He said he wished the "ramblings of crazy people didn't in any way resemble how we actually talk to each other on television". Before commercial break, Stewart told viewers that the show would continue as usual the next night. After commercial break, the show featured a rerun of a field piece done by Jason Jones two years earlier.

The New York Times opined that he is "the modern-day equivalent of Edward R. Murrow" and the UK national newspaper The Independent called him the "satirist-in-chief". In an interview, Senator John McCain described Stewart as "a modern-day Will Rogers and Mark Twain".

Wyatt Cenac said that Stewart cursed him out after Cenac acknowledged he was uncomfortable about a June 2011 Daily Show bit about Republican Presidential candidate Herman Cain .

In March 2013, it was announced that Stewart would be taking a 12-week hiatus from The Daily Show to direct the film Rosewater, based on the book Then They Came for Me by Maziar Bahari. Beginning June 10, 2013, The

Daily Show correspondent John Oliver assumed primary hosting duties during Stewart's break. TV Guide's annual survey for 2013 star salaries showed that Stewart is the highest-paid late night host, making an estimated $25–30 million per year.

On July 14, 2014, Stewart interviewed Hillary Clinton about the Middle East. Clinton's condemnations of Hamas led Stewart to ask her: "But don't you think they would look at that though as, they've given a lot of different things a chance and these are the only guys to them that are giving any resistance to what their condition is?" For Gazans living in that situation, he said Hamas could be viewed as "freedom fighters". On August 1, 2014, Stewart stated on air that "We cannot be Israel's rehab sponsor and its drug dealer".

During a taping of the show on February 10, 2015, Stewart announced he was leaving The Daily Show. Comedy Central President Michele Ganeless confirmed Stewart's retirement with a statement. It was later announced that South African comedian Trevor Noah would succeed Stewart as the host of the show. On April 20, 2015, Stewart indicated that his final show would be on August 6, 2015.

On July 28, 2015, Darren Samuelsohn of Politico reported that Stewart had been twice at the White House for previously unreported meetings with President Obama: once in October 2011 and once in February 2014. Michael D. Shear of The New York Times also picked up on the story. Stewart responded on his show by pointing out that the meetings were listed in the President's publicly available visitor log and that he has been asked to meet privately by many prominent individuals including Roger Ailes of Fox News. He said Obama encouraged him not to make young Americans cynical about their government, and Stewart replied that he was actually "skeptically idealistic".

The hour-plus-long final show on August 6 featured reunions with former Daily Show correspondents and cameo video clips from people Stewart had targeted over the years including Bill O'Reilly, John McCain, Chris Christie, and Hillary Clinton. It concluded with a performance by Bruce Springsteen and the E Street Band.

In November 2015, it was announced that Stewart signed a four-year deal with HBO that will include exclusive digital content for HBO NOW, HBO Go and other platforms.

In 1998, Stewart released his first book, Naked Pictures of Famous People, a collection of humorous short stories and essays. The book reached The New York Times Best Seller List.

In 2004, Stewart and The Daily Show writing staff released America : A Citizen's Guide to Democracy Inaction, a mock high school History textbook offering insights into the unique American system of government, dissecting its institutions, explaining its history and processes, and satirizing such popular American political precepts as "one man, one vote", "government by the people," and "every vote counts." The book sold millions of copies upon its 2004 release and ended the year as a top-fifteen best seller.

In 2005, Stewart provided the voice of President James A. Garfield for the audiobook version of Sarah Vowell's Assassination Vacation.

In 2007, Stewart voiced a role on Stephen Colbert's audiobook version of I Am America . He plays Mort Sinclaire, former TV comedy writer and Communist.

On September 21, 2010, Earth : A Visitor's Guide to the Human Race, written by Stewart and other writers of The Daily Show, was released.

In March 2012, Stewart interviewed Bruce Springsteen for Rolling Stone.

Although best known for his work on The Daily Show, Stewart has had roles in several films and television series. His first film role was a bit part in the box-office bomb Mixed Nuts. He landed a minor part in The First Wives Club, but his scene was deleted. In 1995, Stewart signed a three-year deal with Miramax. He played romantic leads in the films Playing by Heart and Wishful Thinking. He had a supporting role in the romantic comedy Since You've Been Gone and in the horror film The Faculty. Other films were planned for Stewart to write and star in, but they were never produced. Stewart has since maintained a relationship with Miramax founders Harvey and Bob Weinstein and continues to appear in films they have produced including Jay and Silent Bob Strike Back, Doogal and the documentary Wordplay.

He appeared in Half Baked as an "enhancement smoker" and in Big Daddy as Adam Sandler's roommate; he has joked on the Daily Show and in the documentary The Aristocrats that to get the role he slept with Sandler. Stewart often makes fun of his appearances in the high-profile flop Death to Smoochy, in which he played a treacherous television executive, and the animated film Doogal, where he played a blue spring named Zeebad who shot a freeze ray from his mustache. In 2007, Stewart made a cameo appearance as himself in Evan Almighty, which starred former Daily Show correspondent Steve Carell. In the movie, Stewart was seen on a television screen in a fictional Daily Show episode poking fun at Carell's character for building an ark.

Stewart had a recurring role in The Larry Sanders Show, playing himself as an occasional substitute and possible successor to late-night talk show host Larry Sanders . In 1998, Stewart hosted the television special, Elmopalooza, celebrating 30 years of Sesame Street. He has guest-starred on other sitcoms including The Nanny, Dr. Katz, Professional Therapist, Spin City, NewsRadio, American Dad!, and The Simpsons. He has made guest-appearances on the children's television series Between the Lions, Sesame Street and Jack's Big Music Show.

In the mid-1990s, Stewart launched his own production company, Busboy Productions, naming the company in reference to his previous job as a busboy. Stewart signed a deal with Miramax to develop projects through his company, but none of his ideas have been produced. After Stewart's success as host and producer of The Daily Show, he revived Busboy Productions with Daily Show producers Ben Karlin and Rich Korson. In 2002, Busboy planned to produce a sitcom for NBC starring Stephen Colbert, but the show did not come to fruition.

In 2005, Comedy Central reached an agreement with Busboy in which Comedy Central would provide financial backing for the production company. Comedy Central has a first-look agreement on all projects, after which Busboy is free to shop them to other networks.

The deal spawned the Daily Show spin-off The Colbert Report and its replacement The Nightly Show with Larry Wilmore. Other projects include the sitcom pilot Three Strikes, the documentary Sportsfan, the series Important Things with Demetri Martin, and the film The Donor.

After Stewart's departure from The Daily Show, he was listed as an executive producer on The Late Show with Stephen Colbert.

In March 2010, Stewart announced that he had optioned rights to the story of journalist Maziar Bahari, who was imprisoned in Iran for 118 days. On the June 6, 2011 episode of The Daily Show, Stewart again hosted Bahari, and in March

2013, he announced that he was leaving the show for 12 weeks to direct the film version of Bahari's 2011 book Then They Came For Me. Stewart's screenplay adaptation is titled Rosewater. It premiered at the September 2014 Toronto International Film Festival, receiving "generally favorable" reviews, and was released to general audiences on November 14, 2014.

On directing, Stewart noted on Lazarus's show that "The Daily Show" influenced his directing process more than his acting gigs did. He said, "It's about the collaboration. It's about understanding. Doing a show taught me this process of clarity of vision, but flexibility of process. So know your intention, know where you're wanting to go with the scene with the way that you want it to go, the momentum shifts, the emphasis, where you want it to be." He also expressed interest in directing more films.

Stewart has hosted the Grammy Awards twice, in 2001 and in 2002, and the 78th Academy Awards, which were held March 5 at the Kodak Theatre in Hollywood. Critical response to Stewart's performance was mixed. Roger Ebert compared him favorably to legendary Oscar host Johnny Carson. Other reviewers were less positive; Tom Shales of The Washington Post said that Stewart hosted with "smug humorlessness." James Poniewozik of TIME said that Stewart was a bad host, but a great "anti-host" in that he poked fun at parts of the broadcast that deserved it, which lent him a degree of authenticity with the non-Hollywood audience. Stewart and correspondent John Oliver later poked fun at his lackluster reception on The Daily Show's coverage of the 79th Academy Awards by saying that the "demon of last year's Oscars had finally been exorcised."

Stewart returned to host the 80th Academy Awards on February 24, 2008. The reception to his performance was better received. Matthew Gilbert of the

Boston Globe felt the ceremony itself was average but praised Stewart, writing that, "It was good to see Jon Stewart being Jon Stewart. He is shaping up to be a dependable Oscar host for the post-Billy Crystal years. He's not musical, but he's versatile enough to swing smoothly between jokes about politics, Hollywood, new media, and, most importantly, hair." Variety columnist Brian Lowry lauded Stewart's performance noting that he "earned his keep by maintaining a playful, irreverent tone throughout the night, whether it was jesting about Cate Blanchett's versatility or watching Lawrence of Arabia on an iPhone screen.

In December 2009, Stewart gave a speech at the John F. Kennedy Center for the Performing Arts honoring Bruce Springsteen, one of that year's Kennedy Center Honors recipients, and of whom Stewart is a fan. Stewart gave another speech paying tribute to Springsteen in February 2013 as part of the singer's MusiCares Person of the Year award ceremony.

Stewart began a comedic feud with WWE wrestler Seth Rollins in March 2015, and appeared on WWE Raw during a Daily Show-styled segment hosted by Rollins. On August 23, 2015, Stewart returned to host the WWE's SummerSlam at the Barclays Center in Brooklyn, New York. He would later get involved in the main event between Rollins and John Cena, helping Rollins retain his WWE World Heavyweight Championship, as well as winning Cena's United States Championship. The next night on Raw, he explained his actions, saying he did it for Ric Flair , which was to retain his world championship record. Cena then gave Stewart his finishing move, the Attitude Adjustment, to end the segment. Stewart returned at SummerSlam on August 21, 2016 as a special guest.

Stewart's criticism of television journalists

In a televised exchange with then-CNN correspondent Tucker Carlson on Crossfire on October 15, 2004, Stewart criticized the state of television journalism and pleaded with the show's hosts to "stop hurting America", and referred to both Carlson and co-host Paul Begala as "partisan hacks". When posted on the internet, this exchange became widely viewed and was a topic of much media discussion.

Despite being on the program to comment on current events, Stewart immediately shifted the discussion toward the show itself, asserting that Crossfire had failed in its responsibility to inform and educate viewers about politics as a serious topic. Stewart stated that the show engaged in partisan hackery instead of honest debate, and said that the hosts' assertion that Crossfire is a debate show is like "saying pro wrestling is a show about athletic competition." Carlson responded by saying that Stewart criticizes news organizations for not holding public officials accountable, but when he interviewed John Kerry, Stewart asked a series of "softball" questions . Stewart responded that he didn't realize "the news organizations look to Comedy Central for their cues on integrity." When Carlson continued to press Stewart on the Kerry issue, Stewart said, "You're on CNN! The show that leads into me is puppets making crank phone calls! What is wrong with you?" In response to prods from Carlson, "Come on. Be funny," Stewart said, "No, I'm not going to be your monkey." Later in the show when Carlson jibed, "I do think you're more fun on your show," Stewart retorted, "You're as big a dick on your show as you are on any show." In response to Stewart's criticisms, Carlson said, "You need to get a job at a journalism school," to which Stewart responded, "You need to go to one!"

Stewart discussed the incident on The Daily Show the following Monday:

In January 2005, CNN announced that it was canceling Crossfire. When asked about the cancellation, CNN's incoming president, Jonathan Klein, referenced Stewart's appearance on the show: "I think he made a good point about the noise level of these types of shows, which does nothing to illuminate the issues of the day."

On March 18, 2009, Carlson wrote a blog entry for The Daily Beast criticizing Stewart for his handling of the CNBC controversy . Carlson discussed the CNN incident and claimed that Stewart remained backstage for at least "an hour" and "continued to lecture our staff", something Carlson described as "one of the weirdest things I have ever seen."

Stewart again became a viral internet phenomenon following a March 4, 2009, The Daily Show sequence. CNBC canceled Rick Santelli's scheduled appearance but Stewart still ran a short segment showing CNBC giving bad investment advice.

Subsequent media coverage of exchanges between Jim Cramer, who had been featured heavily in the original segment, and Stewart, led to a highly anticipated face-to-face confrontation on The Daily Show. The episode received much media attention and became the second most-viewed episode of The Daily Show, trailing only the 2009 Inauguration Day episode. It had 2.3 million total viewers, and the next day, the show's website saw its highest day of traffic in 2009. Although Cramer acknowledged on the show that some of Stewart's criticisms of CNBC were valid and that the network could "do better," he later said on The Today Show that Stewart's criticism of the media was "naïve and misleading."

Throughout his tenure on The Daily Show, Stewart has frequently accused Fox News of distorting the news to fit a conservative agenda, at one point ridiculing the network as "the meanest sorority in the world." In November 2009, Stewart called out Fox News for using some footage from a previous Tea Party rally during a report on a more recent rally, making the latter event appear more highly attended than it actually was. The show's anchor, Sean Hannity, apologized for the footage use the following night. A month later, Stewart criticized Fox & Friends cohost Gretchen Carlson – a former Miss America and Stanford graduate – for claiming that she googled words such as "ignoramus" and "czar". Stewart said that Carlson was dumbing herself down for "an audience who sees intellect as an elitist flaw".

Stewart stepped up his criticism of Fox News in 2010; as of April 24, The Daily Show had 24 segments criticizing Fox News' coverage. Bill O'Reilly, host of the talk show The O'Reilly Factor on Fox News, countered that The Daily Show was a "key component of left-wing television" and that Stewart loved Fox News because the network was "not boring".

During an interview with Chris Wallace on June 19, 2011, Stewart called Wallace "insane" after Wallace said that Stewart's earlier comparison of a Sarah Palin campaign video and an anti-herpes medicine ad was a political comment. Stewart also said Fox viewers are the "most consistently misinformed" viewers of political media. This comment was ranked by fact-checking site PolitiFact as false, with conditions. Stewart later accepted his error.

In 2014, Stewart engaged in an extended "call-out" of Fox News based on their perceived hypocritical coverage of food stamps and U.S. Government assistance. This culminated during the Bundy standoff involving multiple segments, across multiple episodes, specifically singling out Sean Hannity and Hannity's coverage of the event. Hannity would "return fire" by calling out Stewart for associating himself with Cat Stevens during his Rally in 2010. Stewart responded to this by calling out Hannity for frequently calling Ted Nugent a "friend and frequent guest" on his program and supporting Nugent's violent rhetoric towards Barack Obama and Hillary Clinton in 2007. In late August 2014, Stewart vehemently opposed the manner in which Fox News portrayed the events surrounding the shooting of teenager Michael Brown by police officer Darren Wilson in Ferguson, Missouri and the subsequent protests from citizens.

Advocacy

Stewart sometimes used The Daily Show to argue for causes such as the treatment of veterans and 9/11 first responders. He is credited with breaking a Senate deadlock over a bill to provide health care and benefits for 9/11 emergency workers; the bill passed three days after he featured a group of 9/11 responders on the show. In March 2009, he criticized a White House proposal to remove veterans from Veterans Administration rolls if they had private health insurance; the White House dropped the plan the next day.

Writers Guild of America strike of 2007–2008

Stewart was an important factor in the unionization of the Comedy Central writers. The Daily Show writers were the first of Comedy Central's writers to be able to join the guild, after which other shows followed.

Stewart supported the 2007–08 Writers Guild of America strike. On The Daily Show episode just before the strike, he sarcastically commented about how Comedy Central had made available all episodes for free on their website, but without advertising, and said, "go support our advertisers". The show went on hiatus when the strike began, as did other late night talk shows. Upon Stewart's return to the show on January 7, 2008, he refused to use the title The Daily Show, stating that The Daily Show was the show made with all of the people responsible for the broadcast, including his writers. During the strike, he referred to his show as A Daily Show with Jon Stewart until the strike ended on February 13, 2008.

Stewart's choice to return to the air did bring criticism that he was undermining the writers of his show. Seth MacFarlane wrote an inside joke into an episode of Family Guy about this, causing Stewart to respond with an hour-long call in which he questioned how MacFarlane could consider himself the "moral arbiter" of Hollywood. Other former writers of The Daily Show such as David Feldman have also indicated that Stewart was anti-union at the time and punished his writers for their decision to unionize.

The Writers Guild Strike of 2007–08 was also responsible for a notable mock feud between Stewart, Stephen Colbert, and Conan O'Brien in early 2008. Without writers to help fuel their banter, the three comedians concocted a crossover/rivalry in order to garner more viewers during the ratings slump. Colbert made the claim that because of "the Colbert bump", he was responsible for Mike Huckabee's success in the 2008 presidential race. O'Brien claimed that he was responsible for Huckabee's success because not only had he mentioned Huckabee on his show, but also that he was responsible for Chuck Norris' success . In response, Stewart claimed that he was responsible for the success of O'Brien, since Stewart had featured him on The Jon Stewart Show, and in turn the success of Huckabee. This resulted in a three-part comedic battle between the three pundits, with all three appearing on each other's shows. The feud ended on Late Night with Conan O'Brien with a mock brawl involving the three hosts.

Influences

Stewart has said his influences include George Carlin, Lenny Bruce, David Letterman, Steve Martin, and Richard Pryor. Among comedians who say they were influenced by Stewart are Stephen Colbert, John Oliver, Larry Wilmore, and Trevor Noah.

Personal life

Stewart is Jewish by ethnicity but is irreligious.

While making the 1997 film Wishful Thinking, a production assistant on the film set Stewart up on a blind date with Tracey Lynn McShane. They dated for four years. Stewart proposed to her through a personalized crossword puzzle created with the help of Will Shortz, the crossword editor at The New York Times. They married in 2000. On June 19, 2001, Stewart and his wife filed a joint name change application and legally changed both of their surnames to "Stewart." With the help of in vitro fertilization, the couple has two children.

In 2000, when he was labeled a Democrat, Stewart generally agreed but described his political affiliation as "more socialist or independent" than Democratic. Stewart has voted for Republicans, the last time being in the 1988 presidential election when he voted for George H. W. Bush over Michael Dukakis. He described Bush as having "an integrity about him that I respected greatly".

In 2013, Jon and Tracey bought a 12-acre farm in Middletown, New Jersey, called "Bufflehead Farm". The Stewarts use it as a sanctuary for abused animals. In 2015 Stewart started a vegetarian diet out of ethical reasons; his wife is a long-time vegan.

Honors and awards

Stewart and other members of The Daily Show have received two Peabody Awards for "Indecision 2000" and "Indecision 2004", covering the 2000 presidential election and the 2004 presidential election, respectively.

The Daily Show received the Primetime Emmy Award for Outstanding Writing for a Variety, Music, or Comedy Program in 2001, 2003, 2004, 2005, 2006, 2009, 2011, 2012, and 2015 and Outstanding Variety, Music, or Comedy Series for 10 consecutive years from 2003 to 2012. In 2013, the award for both categories instead went to The Daily Show spin-off The Colbert Report. In 2015, The Daily Show resurfaced, winning both categories for one last time for Stewart's swan song as host.

Stewart won the Grammy Award for Best Comedy Album in 2005 for his recording, America : A Citizen's Guide to Democracy Inaction.

In the December 2003 New Year's edition of Newsweek, Stewart was named the "Who's Next?" person for 2004, with the magazine predicting that he would emerge as an absolute sensation in that year.

In 2004, Stewart spoke at the commencement ceremonies at his alma mater, William and Mary, and received an honorary Doctor of Arts degree. Stewart was also the Class Day keynote speaker at Princeton University in 2004, and the 2008 Sacerdote Great Names speaker at Hamilton College.

Stewart was named one of the 2005 Time 100, an annual list of 100 of the most influential people of the year by TIME magazine.

Stewart and The Daily Show received the 2005 National Council of Teachers of English George Orwell Award for Distinguished Contribution to Honesty and Clarity in Public Language.

Stewart was presented an Honorary All-America Award by the National Soccer Coaches Association of America in 2006.

On April 21, 2009, President of Liberia Ellen Johnson Sirleaf made Stewart a chief.

On October 26, 2010, Stewart was named the Most Influential Man of 2010 by AskMen.

Bibliography

Comedy Central is an American basic cable and satellite television channel owned by Viacom Music and Entertainment Group, a unit of the Viacom Media Networks division of Viacom. The channel carries comedy programming, in the form of both original and syndicated series and stand-up comedy specials, as well as feature films.

Since early 2000s, Comedy Central has expanded globally with localized channels in Germany, Czech Republic, Hungary, Israel, Italy, Latin America, New Zealand, The Netherlands, Norway, Poland, Spain, Sweden, Denmark, Republic of Ireland, United Kingdom, India, Brazil, Albania, Bosnia and Herzegovina, Bulgaria, Belgium, Croatia, Romania, Macedonia, Montenegro,

Philippines, Serbia, Slovenia, Middle East and Africa. The international channels are operated by Viacom International Media Networks.

As of February 2015, approximately 93,992,000 American households receive Comedy Central.

History

On November 15, 1989, Time Warner, owners of HBO, launched The Comedy Channel as the first cable channel devoted exclusively to comedy-based programming. On April 1, 1990, Viacom launched a rival channel called Ha! that featured reruns of situation comedies and some original sketch comedy.

The Comedy Channel's programs were broadcast from the HBO Downtown Studios at 120 East 23rd Street in Manhattan. The format prior to the merger with Ha! included several original and unconventional programs such as Onion World with Rich Hall and Mystery Science Theater 3000, as well as laid-back variety/talk shows hosted by comedians, including The Sweet Life with Rachel Sweet, Night After Night with Allan Havey, Sports Monster, and The Higgins Boys and Gruber, the latter of whom performed sketches in between showings of vintage television series like Supercar, Clutch Cargo, and Lancelot Link, Secret Chimp.

The standard format for The Comedy Channel's shows usually involved the various hosts introducing clips culled from the acts of stand-up comedians as well as classic comedies of the 1970s and 1980s, such as Young Frankenstein and Kentucky Fried Movie, presented in a style similar to music videos. In the early days, certain hours of the day when clips were shown without "host segments" were dubbed Short Attention Span Theater. In 1990, hosts under this title, Jon Stewart and Patty Rosborough, were introduced. Comedian Marc Maron also hosted the series.

While The Comedy Channel broadcast mostly low-budget original programming, Ha!'s schedule featured sitcom and sketch comedy reruns as well as complete 90-minute reruns of Saturday Night Live from the sixth through 16th seasons.

After two years of limited distribution, the two channels merged into one, relaunching on April 1, 1991 as CTV: The Comedy Network; it later changed its name to Comedy Central on June 1, 1991 to prevent issues with the Canadian broadcast television network CTV, which would eventually be its Canadian content partner through The Comedy Network six years later. Viacom bought out Time Warner's half in April 2003 for $1.23 billion. Despite HBO's exit from the venture, the Viacom Media Networks division in charge of Comedy Central is still called Comedy Partners, currently being a partnership of Viacom International, the operating subsidiary of Viacom of which Viacom Media Networks is a division, and Viacom Hearty Ha! Ha! LLC, the subsidiary that owned Ha! and Viacom's original half of the network.

From the late 1980s through the mid-1990s, much of the programming on Comedy Central and its predecessors consisted of comedy films, sitcom reruns, half-hour specials, and clip shows featuring comedians. With the exception of the cult favorite Mystery Science Theater 3000, the channel had a relatively small viewership. A notable early success was Politically Incorrect with Bill Maher, which after showing promise on Comedy Central was quickly snapped up by ABC. Additionally, The Daily Show had got its start with original host Craig Kilborn, although it would take a few more years for the show to reach high popularity with the introduction of Jon Stewart .

Dr. Katz, Professional Therapist was also a notable original program from this era, as well as the game show Win Ben Stein's Money. Successful non-original programming included Canadian comedy group The Kids in the Hall and British shows such as the U.K. edition of Whose Line Is It Anyway? and the sitcom Absolutely Fabulous. Some later seasons of "AbFab", as it was informally known, were partially financed by Comedy Central. Comedy Central also had the national rights to broadcast reruns of Seattle's Almost Live! between 1992 and 1993.

The channel made a breakthrough when South Park premiered in 1997. Being the first major basic cable show to carry the TV-MA rating for mature audiences, the show was too controversial to be picked up by a mainstream network. As word of mouth spread, the number of people who requested that Comedy Central be added to their cable providers increased, and the channel became available in over 50% of American homes by 1998.

In October 2000, Comedy Central modernized its globe logo, by straightening the buildings and removing the transmitter. The management of the network said that the transmitter of the 1991 logo was said to "communicate the 1950s broadcast era". In 2002, Comedy Central Records was formed as a means of releasing albums by comedians that have appeared on the network.

Since 2003, Comedy Central has created a tradition of roasting comedians in the style of the New York Friars' Club roasts. During these roasts, friends of the roastee, along with other comedians, take turns making fun of the roastee, the other roasters, and occasionally audience members. So far, the roastees have included Denis Leary, Jeff Foxworthy, Pamela Anderson, William Shatner, Flavor Flav, Bob Saget, Larry the Cable Guy, Joan Rivers, Rob Reiner, David

Hasselhoff, Donald Trump, Charlie Sheen, Roseanne Barr, James Franco, Justin Bieber, and Rob Lowe.

The success of South Park, despite its mature content, encouraged the network to continue to push the limits on adult language. Every Saturday and Sunday morning at 1 a.m. ET, a movie, comedy special, or animated program is shown unedited for language as part of a block called the Secret Stash. It premiered on July 4, 2003 with the unedited cable television debut of South Park: Bigger, Longer & Uncut. Though no language is censored on the Secret Stash, most nudity in the programs is still edited out, with the exception of limited nudity allowed in animated programs such as Drawn Together, and rear nudity.

In late 2004, it was reported that the four highest-rated shows on Comedy Central were, in descending order, South Park, Chappelle's Show, The Daily Show and Reno 911!. Shortly thereafter, Dave Chappelle backed out of the much-anticipated third season of Chappelle's Show. Meanwhile, The Daily Show continued to climb in the ratings. In October 2005, on the occasion of a new three-year contract for South Park and the launch of Daily Show spin-off The Colbert Report, it was reported that South Park and The Daily Show were the two highest-rated shows on Comedy Central. Comedy Central chief Doug Herzog was reported as saying that he hoped to continue to air new seasons of South Park forever, and that The Colbert Report fulfilled a long-held plan to extend the Daily Show brand.

On April 5, 2006, in a controversial two-part episode arc titled "Cartoon Wars Part I" and "Cartoon Wars Part II", South Park touched the issue of the recent protest over the Danish cartoon drawings depicting the Muslim prophet Muhammad. The image of Muhammad did not appear in the episode. The episode also mocked fellow cartoon Family Guy. On April 13, 2006, Comedy

Central issued a statement which appears to confirm that the network prohibited the show's creators from airing an image of Muhammad. The statement reads, "In light of recent world events, we feel we made the right decision." An anonymous source close to the show indicated that South Park creators Trey Parker and Matt Stone were informed of the policy several weeks earlier, and wrote this story arc in protest. This was a change of policy for Comedy Central, having allowed South Park to portray an image of Muhammad in an earlier episode, "Super Best Friends". Oddly enough, an image of Muhammad was still briefly visible in the opening credits of the "Cartoon Wars" episodes .

On January 15, 2007, MTV Networks International launched Comedy Central in Germany which is available for free throughout Europe. The channel airs 33 shows either dubbed in German or subtitled while also airing locally produced shows. On April 30, Dutch channel The Box was relaunched as the Dutch version of Comedy Central during the primetime and overnight hours timesharing with Nickelodeon. On May 1, 2007, Comedy Central expanded to Italy, replacing Paramount Comedy.

On June 27, 2007, CTVglobemedia-owned networks CTV and The Comedy Network obtained the exclusive Canadian rights to the entire Comedy Central library of past and current programs on all electronic platforms, under a multi-year agreement with Viacom, expanding on past programming agreements between the two channels. Canadian users attempting to visit Comedy Central websites were redirected to The Comedy Network's website. The Canadian channel retains its own brand name, but the agreement is otherwise very similar to the earlier CTV/Viacom deal for MTV in Canada. As of 2011, this geocaching no longer applies and both the Comedy Central and The Comedy

Network websites can be accessed worldwide, with the exception of videos which remain only accessible within each respective country.

In December 2007, Comedy Central picked up a show hosted by Lewis Black called Lewis Black's Root of All Evil, which debuted in March 2008. On January 9, 2008, it was announced the Comedy Central and MTV would allow the streaming its programs online for free starting in February of that year. On January 24, Scott Landsman became the Vice President of Original Programming and Development at the network.

On March 27, 2008, the Swedish Radio and TV Authority approved an application from Comedy Central regarding being allowed to air television programs in Sweden. The grant allows Comedy Central to broadcast on the terrestrial television network between January 1, 2009 and March 31, 2014, after which a new request must be submitted in order to continue broadcasting. Comedy Central's U.S. flagship network picked up a remake of The Gong Show hosted by Dave Attell, star of his former self-titled Comedy Central series Insomniac, which debuted in July 2008. Another new show called Reality Bites Back premiered after The Gong Show with Dave Attell.

In June 2008, Comedy Central picked up the sketch comedy show Important Things with Demetri Martin, which began airing in February 2009. On April 1, 2009, Comedy Central began airing in New Zealand as channel 010 on SKY Digital. On April 6, Paramount Comedy in the UK and Ireland rebranded as Comedy Central. On April 7, 2009, it was announced Comedy Central would air new stand-up comedy specials starring Christopher Titus, Gabriel Iglesias, Pablo Francisco, Jim Breuer, Mitch Fatel and Pete Correale, and ventriloquist Jeff Dunham. An animated show entitled Ugly Americans was also picked up by the network. In 2009, The Goode Family premiered. Also in 2009, Thomas

Lennon announced via Twitter that Reno 911! had been cancelled after six seasons, much to fan disapproval. The network also played a role in the revival of the animated series Futurama, which Fox had cancelled in 2003. New episodes began airing on Comedy Central in 2010. But in May 2013, Comedy Central released a statement saying that the contract between Futurama and Comedy Central would not be renewed, and that the summer of 2013 would be Futurama's final season on the air. However, episodes continue to run daily on Comedy Central.

South Park episodes "200" and "201" aired in April 2010, revisiting the issue of the Islamic religious figure Muhammad's perceived immunity to parody, for fear of violent retaliation. The Super Best Friends returned, but Muhammad was entirely covered by a black bar reading "CENSORED" through all of his screen time. By the second episode of the two-parter, Comedy Central decided to censor every instance of his name, as well as three entire monologues, from the end of the show. The monologues dealt with the subjects of censorship and intimidation, but did not actually use Muhammad's name. Parker and Stone have since issued a statement to the press, confirming that the "bleeps" were added weeks after the show was finished, and that Comedy Central has refused to let them post the original version to South Park Studios, in addition to retroactively removing the original "Super Best Friends" episode.

On December 10, 2010, Comedy Central introduced a new logo for the network that launched on January 1, 2011, which left behind the previous theme of a world-sized "tower" broadcasting the network/skyscrapers, in favor of an image of two "C"'s, with one of them and the word "Central" turned upside-down within the new logomark. The new logo was designed to represent the network's unique brand of comedy , and to provide the network with a logo that could be easily used across different platforms, such as social media. The logo's resemblance to the one used by the Federal Communications Commission has also been pointed out. It went on to win several industry awards. The company also standardised its publicity material and idents to use the fonts Brandon Grotesque and Eames Century Modern.

The Polish version of the channel was the first international Comedy Central channel to switch to the new logo on February 20, 2011; followed by the Hungarian version on April 1, 2011. Versions of the channel in Germany and the Netherlands soon followed on October 1, 2011. Comedy Central New Zealand rebranded in April 2012. Viacom 18 launched the channel in India on January 23, 2012. StarHub launched Comedy Central Asia in Singapore on November 1, 2012; the channel was added to its Basic Entertainment Upsize group.

On October 21, 2013, the network premiered a nightly comedy-game show series @midnight hosted by Chris Hardwick. @midnight serves as an expansion to the network's nightly late-night programming.

In 2014, it was announced that Stephen Colbert would leave Comedy Central to host Late Show with Stephen Colbert on CBS, following the retirement of David Letterman, the first host of Late Show. The final episode of The Colbert Report aired on Comedy Central on December 18, 2014, after nine years and a total of 1,447 episodes. The final episode of The Colbert Report was watched by 2.481 million viewers, making it the most watched episode ever in the show's history. The finale was the most watched cable program of the night in its time slot, beating The Daily Show which was seen by 2.032 million viewers. The Colbert Report was replaced on Comedy Central by Larry Wilmore from

The Daily Show, who began hosting his series The Nightly Show with Larry Wilmore on January 19, 2015 through August 2016 due to low ratings.

On February 10, 2015, Jon Stewart announced that he would retire from hosting The Daily Show, after 16 years of hosting. Stewart's final show aired on August 6, 2015 as a 52-minute special. Trevor Noah began hosting the series on September 28, 2015.

High definition channels and service

The 1080i high definition simulcast feed of Comedy Central launched in 2009 and is available on all major cable and satellite providers.

Criticism

Comedy Central has been a frequent target of criticism from the conservative group Parents Television Council, which accuses them of bigotry and blasphemy, especially within the programs South Park, The Sarah Silverman Program, Halfway Home, and the annual "Roast" special. The PTC has used their criticisms against Comedy Central for their support of the Family and Consumer Choice Act of 2007, which would allow American cable television subscribers to choose which channels they subscribe to and impose the same decency standards that are already in place on broadcast TV, and to persuade advertisers to stop advertising on the channel. PTC founder and former president L. Brent Bozell III has called the channel unfunny, claiming the channel has managed "to reach the top of its field in spite of – or, better put, because of – the network's sheer lack of comedic talent" by its "extensive reliance on shocking or disgusting humor". The PTC criticized the channel for airing advertisements for "Girls Gone Wild". The channel airs the least censored version of the film Not Another Teen Movie, as well as uncut versions of films such as Coming to America, Dogma and Jay and Silent Bob Strike Back.

On November 5, 2007, an open letter was written by VideoSift to protesting the blocking of Comedy Central's embedded video content for non-U.S. based viewers.

On April 21, 2010, Comedy Central censored the South Park episode, "201", in response to a death threat issued by users of a radical Muslim website over the episode's planned depiction of the Islamic prophet Muhammad, which led several newspaper columnists to condemn the network's actions as tantamount to abetting terrorism. As a result, "201" and the episode that preceded it were heavily edited and not shown in repeats.

Printed in Great Britain
by Amazon